DATE DUE		
SEP 2 2004		
SEP 1 2 2005		
OCT 2 1 2005		

DATE DUE		

The Rat, the Ox, and the Zodiac

A Chinese Legend adapted by

DOROTHY VAN WOERKOM

Illustrated by

ERROL LE CAIN

CROWN PUBLISHERS, INC., NEW YORK

For Helen

Published simultaneously in Canada by General Publishing Company Limited
First Edition

The text of this book is set in 14 pt. Garamond No. 3
The illustrations are 4/color pre-separated ink and wash drawings with wash
overlays, reproduced in halftone.

Library of Congress Cataloging in Publication Data

Van Woerkom, Dorothy.
    The rat, the ox, and the zodiac.

    SUMMARY: Recounts how the Rat came to be the animal representing the
first year of the Chinese zodiac.
    [1. Folklore—China]   I. Le Cain, Errol.   II. Title.
PZ8.1.V457Rat   [398.2]   [E]   75-6525   ISBN 0-517-51849-X

THE ANIMALS IN THE CHINESE ZODIAC

There are twelve animals in the Chinese zodiac. The Chinese calendar is divided into twelve-year cycles. Each year of the cycle is named for one of the zodiac animals. The first year is "The Year of the Rat." The second is "The Year of the Ox."

This might have been just the other way around if it had not been for the events in this story.

THE EMPEROR OF CHINA WAS AN UNHAPPY MAN. He sat on his throne facing south, as was the custom.

Before him on a cushion sat a creature who was half-god, half-human. He was a demigod.

A rat crouched on one side of the demigod, and on the other stood an ox.

"Shun Yü," said the emperor to the demigod, "you have chosen the twelve animals for our new zodiac. What is the trouble now?"

Shun Yü's head touched his knees in a bow. "The zodiac animals look to the future, Mighty One. They have decided that all disagreements among them shall be settled by the Beast of the First Year."

"A wise decision," the emperor agreed. "But which of the twelve shall be first?"

Ox hurried forward and bowed to the emperor. "Oh, Lord of the Middle Kingdom!" he cried. "The other beasts will listen to *me,* because I am so big and strong."

Rat stood where he was, but he tried to touch his knees with his head as he had seen the demigod do.

"Lord of our Zodiac," said Rat, "the other beasts will listen to *me,* because I am so clever and wise."

The emperor sighed. He stretched out his arm, and the long yellow sleeve of his robe touched the floor tiles.

"Are the other beasts satisfied with their places in the zodiac?" he asked Shun Yü.

The demigod nodded his head. Ox and Rat nodded, too.

"Then," said the Emperor, "let the other ten decide whether Ox or Rat shall be first."

Shun Yü set out at once to do as the emperor commanded. In the palace courtyard he met Dog sunning herself. Now, Dog was last-but-one in the new zodiac.

"Do you mind that you are last-but-one in the zodiac?" Shun Yü asked Dog.

"Certainly not," was Dog's reply. "I am honored to be anywhere at all, since only twelve were chosen."

"Which, then, should be first? Ox because he is strong, or Rat because he is wise?"

Dog was small. She feared big Ox might be a big bully. "Rat, of course," she told the demigod.

Shun Yü wrote this on his clay tablet.

At the gate he saw Cock riding on a wagonload of straw.

"Do you mind that you are last-but-two in the new zodiac?" asked Shun Yü of Cock.

"Not at all," said Cock. "Anywhere will do, since only twelve were chosen."

"Then tell me this. Should Rat be first, or Ox? Rat claims the place for his wisdom. Ox claims the place for his strength."

Now, long and long ago Cock had had beautiful horns. Although he lost them through an act of kindness, he missed them every day of his life.

He much admired the horns of Ox, and so he said, "Ox, of course. The Beast of the First Year should be strong."

Shun Yü wrote again on his tablet. He walked until he reached a lake. A stone bridge crossed the lake and Boar stood on the bridge.

The demigod called to him. "Boar! Do you mind that you are last of all in the new zodiac?"

"Not in the least. Only twelve were chosen, I am told."

"Rat and Ox are quarreling," Shun Yü said. "Both want to be first. Rat says First Beast should be wise. Ox says First Beast should be strong."

"Rat thinks too much of himself," cried Boar. "What *is* wise, after all? Do you know? Do I know? Let Ox be first."

Shun Yü wrote this on his tablet. He walked on until he came to the rain forest. There he met Tiger, third beast in the zodiac.

"Friend Tiger! Do you mind that you are last-but-nine in the new zodiac?"

"No, as a matter of fact. To be one of twelve is honor enough."

"Well, then," said the demigod. "Ox thinks he should be first, for he is strong. Rat thinks he should be first, for he is wise."

Tiger was a clever beast and smart. How clever Rat must be to think that he could challenge Ox!

"Rat, of course," was Tiger's reply.

"I disagree!" came a voice from above. It belonged to Monkey. "Anyone can see that Ox is strong," he said, "but who can show that Rat is wise?"

"You are a fool, friend Monkey," hissed Snake who was near Shun Yü's feet. Snake uncoiled herself and rose as high as the demigod's sash.

"I am last-but-six, which matters not at all. But a First Beast who is wise is better than a First Beast who is strong."

Shun Yü wrote this down. He followed the path to the edge of the rain forest and into the meadow beyond it. Sheep was lying in the shade.

"Friend Sheep," said Shun Yü, "do you mind that you are last-but-four in the new zodiac?"

"How can you ask that?" Sheep demanded. "After all, only twelve were chosen."

"Another question, Sheep. Both Ox and Rat demand first place. Ox for his powerful body. Rat for his clever brain."

Now, Sheep cared little for hustle and bustle, or hurry and scurry. A clever creature like Rat must hustle and scurry most of the time.

"Ox," said Sheep.

Horse, who was last-but-five, galloped up. "Do not listen to her," he said. "Ox could be as smart as Rat, but he is too lazy to use his brain."

"I agree!" cried Rabbit as he hopped over Sheep and landed next to Horse. "Ox hates to think. He only likes to look big. But Rat uses his brain every single day."

Shun Yü nodded to Rabbit. "You are last-but-eight. And you and Horse have chosen Rat." The demigod wrote this down as he spoke.

There was none left now to ask but Dragon, who lived beneath a rock in the middle of a stream. Shun Yü found the rock and tapped on it with his stylus.

There was a flash of fire, a terrible roar. The water hissed in the stream. The rock rumbled. Dragon appeared, towering over Shun Yü.

Even Shun Yü, demigod that he was, stood in awe of Dragon. It was almost a minute before he found his voice.

"Friend Dragon, do you mind that you are last-but-seven in the new zodiac?"

"Mind?" The word floated in front of Shun Yü on a tongue of yellow fire. "Are there not but twelve of us? Why should I mind?"

"Then tell me this," said Shun Yü. "Both Rat and Ox want to lead the others. Rat because he is wise. Ox because he is strong."

Ox had once done Dragon a tremendous favor. Remembering this he said, "A wise Rat is not as important as a strong Ox."

So Shun Yü returned to give the emperor his report.

Tiger, Rabbit, and Snake had chosen Rat. So had Horse and Dog.

Sheep and Dragon wanted Ox. So did Monkey, Cock, and Boar. They were equally divided!

"It is so difficult," sighed the emperor, "the world can never decide whether might is best, or reason. Neither can the beasts! But we cannot have *two* first animals in our zodiac."

The emperor sent for Rat and Ox. They heard the demigod's report in silence.

Then Ox came forward, bowing low before the emperor. "Lord of the Middle Kingdom! You can see that I am big and strong. How can Rat, who weighs but a few pounds, keep the other beasts from quarreling?"

Rat approached the throne. He bowed so low his whiskers swept the floor.

"It is true, Lord of the Zodiac, that I am only a rat. But everyone thinks his own size and talents best. I am willing to show Ox that brains can sometimes do what size cannot."

"Well, Shun Yü?" said the emperor to the demigod. "How shall we settle this?"

"Put it to the people, Mighty One. While it is true that the Beast of the First Year will rule the other beasts of the zodiac, the zodiac does belong to the people."

"It shall be so!" the emperor cried. "Rat and Ox must show themselves around the city."

Ox agreed. His horns and head bobbed up and down. He knew what the people would say!

But Rat fell down on his knees. He buried his head in his paws and wept.

"Of course we can go into the city," he moaned, "but unless I am just a *little* bigger, no one will even see me walking in Ox's shadow."

Rat peeked to see if Shun Yü was listening. Then he cried again.

"If I were a demigod instead of a rat," he whined, "I would use my magic powers to make me larger!"

"Well," said Shun Yü to Ox, "I can double Rat's size. Then everyone could see him."

Ox did not object. He would still be one hundred times as large as Rat.

So the demigod said the magic words and Rat grew larger. Then Rat and Ox went out into the city.

"Look!" someone shouted. "Never have I seen such a great rat."

"Did you ever see such a rat?" asked another.

"See the huge rat!" shouted one to another.

Down the streets and up walked Rat and Ox. Everywhere they went, the people wondered at the huge rat.

But no one even noticed Ox for they saw oxen every day.

Never in their lives had they seen one rat grown as big as two.

Then Shun Yü asked the people if the rat they had seen should be first in the new zodiac, or the ox.

They looked at him in surprise.

"What ox?" they asked. "We only saw a rat. A huge rat!"

And that was how Ox became last-but-ten in the Chinese zodiac. First place went to Rat, who had been wise enough to win it.